Secrets

Every Mother Should Tell Her Daughter About

Life!

by Dr. Mattie Nottage

Secrets Every Mother Should Tell Her Daughter About Life

Copyright © 2014
Mattie Nottage Ministries, Int'l

Secrets Every Mother Should Tell Her Daughter About Life
by Mattie M. Nottage

Printed in the United States of America
ISBN-13: 978-0-9896003-3-0

Unless otherwise indicated, all Scripture quotations are taken from the King James Study Bible ©1988 by Liberty University: Thomas Nelson Publishers, Nashville and The Amplified Bible ©1987 by the Zondervan Corporation and the Lockman Foundation, Grand Rapids, Michigan

Secrets Every Mother Should Tell Her Daughter About Life

*W*ho can find a virtuous woman? for her price is far above rubies.

(Proverbs 31:10)

𝒟edicated to ....

my dearest Magyn, Melissa, Sam, Deandra, Dearyl, my *Girls of Excellence Program*, *Faith Village For Girls Transformation & Empowerment Initiative* and the long list of beautiful women who call me "Mother."

#MOTHERSSECRETS

Why "SECRETS!"

Many years ago I started an after school program mentoring young girls that were socially challenged and deemed "at risk." I called them my "Girls of Excellence". What I did not know at the time was that God had given me the esteemed privilege of impacting the lives of future nurses, doctors, teachers and entrepreneurs.

After seeing the miracle that took place in the life of those girls, The Holy Spirit led me to launch an all-girls transformation and empowerment initiative in my country The Bahamas, called *The Faith Village For Girls Transformation & Empowerment Program*.

During the program, my mandate was to recondition their mindsets, attitudes and their outlook on life. Many of these girls suffered from low self esteem, abuse, rejection and felt as though they had no purpose in life. I built a character development module based on life essential skills and each day I spent time pouring "power" nuggets into their spirits.

Secrets Every Mother Should Tell Her Daughter About Life

These nuggets were the same words I shared with my own daughters as I was preparing them for the game I called "Life." By the end of stage one of the initial program, I realized that these girls were totally transformed into graceful, beautiful young ladies who were ready to embrace God's plan for their lives.

As I saw the transformation that took place in these young ladies, I wanted to impart some of the same "power" nuggets into the lives of other young women everywhere. From the quiet recesses of my own daughters' bedrooms to the hearts of young girls whom I have mentored, I now present a "SECRETS" treasure chest that is able to bring transformation and empowerment to any young lady who is willing to face the daily challenges of life.

From my heart to yours I share with you *"Secrets Every Mother Should Tell Her Daughter About Life!"*

With Love,
Dr. Mattie Nottage

To My Precious, Darling Daughter...

Name: _____

_____

_____

_____

_____

_____

From: _____

Date: _____

Secret #1

Always remember, and never forget ... you are so special! I love and celebrate you for the gem that you are. Stay focused, stay true to God and stay true to yourself!

#STAYTRUE

I will praise thee; for I am fearfully and wonderfully made ...
Psalm 139:14

$\mathscr{S}$ecret #2

$\mathcal{D}$o not allow anyone or anything to get in your pathway of success! Set your goals in life. Lock into your target and go after it!

#YOURPATHWAYOFSUCCESS

I press towards the mark for the prize of the high calling of God in Christ Jesus. – **Philippians 3:14**

*S*ecret #3

*M*ost men want the same thing from every woman.
Never give your heart to a man except you're sure you want to spend the rest of your life with him. If you're not sure then hold on to your heart!

#KEEPYOURHEART

Keep thy heart with all diligence; for out of it are the issues of life. – **Proverbs 4:23**

Secret #4

Assess all of your relationships, friendships, and associations. Enhance those that are valuable and release those that are seemingly not going anywhere. Remember, relationships do matter ... it's the good ones you should fight to maintain.

#RELATIONSHIPS

" ... get to know those who labor among you [recognize them for what they are, acknowledge and appreciate and respect them all] ..." – **1 Thessalonians 5:12**

Secret #5

Do not depend on a man to tell you who you are or what you are good for in life.
See beauty inside of yourself and accept whatever compliment stumbles to you along the way.

#BEAUTYINSIDE

Thou are all fair (beautiful), my love; there is no spot in thee.
Song of Solomon 4:7

Secret #6

Do not minimize your moments of success or celebration to make others happy. Enjoy your moment! After all, you earned it.

#ENJOYYOURMOMENTS

And he shall be like a tree planted by the rivers of water, and ... whatsoever he doeth shall prosper. – **Psalm 1:3**

Secret #7

*I*f you see yourself as priceless, you will never be "bought or sold" by anyone. In other words, you must value yourself and others will value you.

#PRICELESS

But [you] are a chosen generation, a royal priesthood, an holy nation, a peculiar people ... - **1 Peter 2:9**

$\mathscr{S}$ecret #8

$\mathcal{N}$ever say, "I Do," until you're sure, very sure, or SURE! SURE! SURE! In other words, be "SURE" to the third degree...(sure³)

#ABSOLUTELYSURE

And the Lord God said, ... I will make him an help meet (suitable) for him. - **Genesis 2:18**

$\mathcal{S}$ecret #9

$\mathbf{S}$eize every door of opportunity...go through it with boldness. DO NOT PROCRASTINATE! Doors open but they can also close.

#SEIZEOPPORTUNITIES

Making the very most of the time [buying up each opportunity], because the days are evil.
Ephesians 5:16 AMP

*S*ecret #10

*P*rocrastination is expensive, and will cost too much to pay for *later*. Do everything in the time allotted. Do not waste a minute, make good on every opportunity.

#PROCRASTINATION

Ye a little sleep, a little slumber, a little folding of the hands to sleep: So shall thy poverty come ... as an armed man.
Proverbs 6:10, 11

$\mathscr{S}$ecret #11

One thing I've learned about "opportunity"... it never runs you down. It presents itself and waits to be noticed.

#NOTICEOPPORTUNITIES

"Behave yourselves wisely [living prudently and with discretion] ... making the very most of the time *and* seizing (buying up) the opportunity." – **Colossians 4:5**

$\mathscr{S}$ecret #12

Opportunity is a chance or prospect to make good in a given situation!

#MAKEGOOD

... now is the acceptable time ... making the very most of the time [buying up each opportunity]
2 Corinthians 6:2a; Ephesians 5:16a

Secret #13

*B*eing a virgin is a good thing. Never allow anyone to belittle or humiliate you because you choose to save yourself for marriage. After all, your virginity is the "token of purity" God gave you – guard it with your life.

#SAVEYOURSELF4MARRIAGE

For this is the will of God, your sanctification: that you abstain from sexual immorality; fornication. – **1 Thessalonians 4:3**

Secret #14

When you know "it" is God...*DO IT!!* If you are not sure – *WAIT!*

#JUSTDOIT!

Nevertheless at thy word I will ....
Luke 5:5

*S*ecret #15

*P*rocrastination is an adversary. Do not play with him. He will waste your time!

#DONOTWASTETIME

See then that you walk circumspectly, not as fools but wise, redeeming the time ... **– Ephesians 5:15 – 16**

Secret #16

*H*aving sex with someone who is not your husband simply means, you have lowered your standards, and have "sold yourself short!"

#STANDARDS

Nevertheless, [to avoid] fornication, let every man have his own wife, and let every woman have her own husband.
1 Corinthians 7:2

Secret #17

Do not let people lead you where you do not want to go!

#DONOTBEMISLED

Do not be deceived: "Bad company corrupts good morals.
1 Corinthians 15:33

ecret #18

Seek God for the man you should fall in love with, marry and maybe someday, prayerfully start a family.
God is unlimited and will only give you your heart's desire.

#SEEKGOD

Delight thyself also in the LORD; and he shall give thee the desires of thine heart. – **Proverbs 37:4**

Secret #19

Commitment and dedication to God will take you EVERYWHERE. Trusting in and depending on people will lead you NOWHERE!

#DEDICATIONTOGOD

Commit thy works unto the Lord and the thoughts shall be established. – **Proverbs 16:3**

*S*ecret #20

*F*irst, love God more than you love anyone in this whole world. Second, love yourself! Then, loving the man you call your husband will come easy.

#LOVE

Jesus said unto him, "Thou shalt love the Lord thy God with all thy heart and with all thy soul, and with all thy mind.
Matthew 22:37

Secret #21

*I*f a man forgets your birthday, he will probably forget your anniversary too!
Hint, Hint – "true love never forgets!"

#NEVERFORGET

... love covers a multitude of sins [forgives and disregards the offenses of others]. – **1 Peter 4:8 AMP**

Secret #22

Release those people who have no intentions of changing. If they are not an asset today they will certainly be a liability tomorrow.

#RELEASEPEOPLE

Be ye not unequally yoked with unbelievers: for what fellowship hath righteousness with unrighteousness, light with darkness? – **2 Corinthians 6:14**

*S*ecret #23

*D*o not allow anyone to abuse you! Physical, mental, verbal, emotional, or sexual abuse is unacceptable, and should not be tolerated. Pray, forgive and, if necessary, find the courage to walk away. Never feel obligated to stay long enough to become a victim.

#WALKAWAYFROMABUSE

As for a man who stirs up division, after warning him once and then twice, have nothing more to do with him .... – **Titus 3:10**

Secret #24

Change is necessary for your progress. If you're going to move forward, you must be willing to embrace change.

#CHANGE4PROGRESS

... be ye transformed by the renewing of your mind ...
Romans 12:2

*S*ecret #25

*L*earn how to cook, clean, iron and change your own car's flat tire. Personal independence is powerful, and should never be mistaken as female dominance. Gracefully celebrate being a woman, and decide to be the **best** woman you can be.

#PERSONALINDEPENDENCE

A good woman is hard to find, and worth far more than diamonds. – **Proverbs 31:10**

Secret #26

Adverse situations sometimes position you for success. Weather your storms carefully. Use the winds to blow your sail to the other side.
"Behind every dark cloud is a silver lining."

#ADVERSESITUATIONS

And we know that all things work together for good to them that love God.... – **Romans 8:28**

*S*ecret #27

*L*earn the 3-W's which govern the "PURPOSE FACTORS" of life!

Know *W*ho you are.
*W*hy are you here?
*W*here are you going?

#3WPURPOSEFACTORS

By having the eyes of your understanding enlightened, you can know and understand the hope to which He has called you...
Ephesians 1:18

$\mathcal{S}$ecret #28

$\mathcal{D}$o not complain ... use opposition to "SET YOUR SAIL" in the direction you really want to go. The stronger the winds blow, the sooner you will reach the other side.

#USEOPPOSITION

For I consider that the sufferings of the present time (present life) are not worth being compared with the glory that is about to be revealed to us. **– Romans 8:18**

Secret #29

*I*f for some strange reason you make a mistake, or fall ... GET UP!
NEVER STAY DOWN!
The seal of champions is in their ability to "bounce back" after they have been knocked down.
You are a champion.
Get up and get back in the fight!

#GETBACKINTHEFIGHT

And let us not grow weary of doing good, for in due season we will reap, if we do not give up. – **Galatians 6:9**

$\mathcal{S}$ecret #30

Crosswinds sometimes act as a catalyst to your destination. Learn to discern your environment and don't curse the change in your atmosphere.

#CROSSWINDS

Be ye steadfast, unmovable, always abounding in the work of the Lord... – **1 Corinthians 15:58**

*S*ecret #31

*T*he female is one of the most peculiar species God created. Celebrate your femininity, and enjoy all the pleasantries that come with being a woman. Trying to change that will only lead you to *complexity, frustration* and *internal warfare.*

#CELEBRATEWOMANHOOD

You made all the delicate, inner parts of my body and knit me together in my mother's womb. – **Psalm 139:13**

*S*ecret #32

*D*on't allow people's negative opinion of you to cloud your mind. Remember you are who you are by the grace of God and that is who you will always be!

#BYGODSGRACE

By the grace (the unmerited favor and blessing) of God I am what I am .... – **1 Corinthians 15:10**

Secret #33

Critique yourself.
Analyze your strengths, and weaknesses. Make the necessary adjustments for change. *Self-analysis* mirrors your true perception of yourself even when no one is looking.

#SELFANALYSIS

Let every person carefully scrutinize and examine and test his own conduct and his own work. – **Galatians 6:4**

ecret #34

Only take advice from people that have walked that road before. Listening to inexperienced novices will lead you in "pot holes", pitfalls and unbelievable dead-ends.

#TAKINGADVICE

The way of fools seems right to them, but the wise listen to godly advice. – **Proverbs 12:15**

$\mathscr{S}$ecret #35

If no-one applauds you for what you felt was a stellar performance, find a mirror and applaud yourself. Be your #1 fan.

#YOURNUMBER1FAN

... but David encouraged himself in the LORD his God...
1 Samuel 30:6

*S*ecret #36

*D*o not be disturbed by facial expressions. Whether people clap or not, keep dancing!
At the time, they may become mesmerized by what they see and withhold their applause. However, after the lights have gone out, they will respond with a standing ovation.

#KEEPDANCING

Then shall the young women rejoice in the dance ...
Jeremiah 31:13

Secret #37

Weigh your options!
Do not settle for crumbs, even if it's FREE!!
Be prepared to pay for things that are of great value.   God has His very best in store for you.

#DONOTSETTLE

... No, ... but I will buy it of you for a price. I will not offer burnt offerings to the Lord my God of that which costs me nothing ...
2 Samuel 24:24

Secret #38

Never compromise your standards to merchandise your gift. Remember it's a gift that God gave you and He should always get the glory from it.

#NEVERCOMPROMISE

Your gift will make room for you and set you before great men.
- **Proverbs 18:16**

Secret #39

Anything that's worth doing in life, if you add value to it, you can do it!

Value = time, effort, investment, energy, commitment, money, worth, faith, dedication, priority.

#WORTHANDVALUE

[Be] not slothful in business; fervent in spirit; ...
– **Romans. 12:11**

Secret #40

Always make time to pamper yourself. Relax and find at least one day to unwind.
Real women all around the world take time for themselves and they tend to live longer.

#PAMPERYOURSELF

And He said to them, "Come away by yourselves to a lonely place and rest a while." - **Mark 6:31**

*S*ecret #41

*E*agles fly high! Others waste time pecking and chirping over bird droppings. Decide whether you are in the company of eagles, or in the circle of "others!" I'd rather be a high-flying eagle than a low-pecking chicken.

#YOUAREANEAGLE

"But they that wait upon the LORD shall renew their strength; they shall mount up with wings as eagles; ..." - **Isaiah 40:31**

*S*ecret #42

*E*xercise discretion in your everyday life. Be cautious of people with whom you surround yourself, especially those called "friends."
Personal prudence should take precedence in everything that you do.

#PERSONALPRUDENCE

"I, Wisdom ... make prudence my dwelling ...."
– Proverbs 8:12 AMP

Secret #43

Foolish people are always overly anxious, wasting time and expending unnecessary energies. Patience is a virtue. Pursue it, and you will have POWER!

#PATIENCEVIRTUEPOWER

"But let patience have her perfect work, that ye may be perfect and entire, wanting nothing." – James 1:4

Secret #44

Giving up is never an option! Perseverance is the order of the day that will eventually lead you to your destiny.

#PERSEVERANCE

For the vision is yet for an appointed time, ...: though it tarry, wait for it; because it will surely come, it will not tarry.
Habakkuk. 2:3

Secret #45

Everyone is not ordained to go with you to the top. Leave some people at the foot of the mountain. Go up and get your gold.
They will be right there on your way back down.

#GETYOURGOLD

Set your affection on things above, not on things on the earth.
Colossians 3:2

Secret #46

You cannot change your past, but you can do everything about your now, and your future.
Your greatest seasons are before you. Move forward!

#FOCUSONYOURFUTURE

...forgetting those things which are behind, and reaching forth unto those things which are before... – **Philippians. 3:13**

Secret #47

Release the past...with great expectation conquer your now and anticipate a great future. Your greatest seasons are before you. Move forward!

#GREATEXPECTATION

"Forget the former things; do not dwell on the past. See I am doing a new thing!" **- Isaiah 43:18-19**

Secret #48

Destiny is where you're headed. Until then, celebrate where you are now!

#YOURDESTINY

"For the vision [is] yet for an appointed time, but at the end it shall speak, and not lie..." - **Habbakuk 2:3**

*S*ecret #49

*T*he *past* is where you were.

*T*he *present* is where you are.

*T*he *future* is where you're going.

Maximize where you are, but spend some prayerful days planning for your great future.

#PASTPRESENTFUTURE

Grace be unto you, and peace, from him which is, and which was, and which is to come ... – **Revelation 1:4**

$\mathscr{S}$ecret #50

$\mathcal{T}$ake time to learn new things.

Glean from people who have experience. If you feel you already know everything, then you are a sad commentary we will all soon read about.

#GLEANFROMOTHERS

A wise [person] will hear, and will increase learning; and a person of understanding shall attain unto wise counsels: - **Proverbs 1:5**

$\mathcal{S}$ecret #51

$\mathcal{D}$on't give people the power to hurt you. Love them, but wear them loose enough so they don't scar you if they disappoint you.

#WEARPEOPLELOOSELY

Put not your trust in princes, nor in the son of man...
– Psalm 146:3

Secret #52

*H*istory and the obituary both speak to your past. Reality speaks to what is, and destiny speaks to what can be. Paint a good picture of what is and paint a portrait of what you would like to be. This image is what you will eventually become.

#WHATYOUBECOME

"Therefore if anyone is in Christ he is a new creation. The old has passed away; the new has come." - **2 Corinthians. 5:17**

Secret #53

*N*ever trust a man or woman more than you trust God. If trusting God is all you can do, then that's all you should do.

#TRUSTGOD

Trust in the Lord with ALL your heart and lean not to your own understanding. – **Proverbs 3:5**

Secret #54

Never open your whole soul to someone unless you have proven their love, loyalty and integrity. Doing so prematurely will only lead to soul-wounds, soul-scars and many "broken pieces."

#LOVEANDINTEGRITY

... neither cast ye your **pearls before swine**, lest they trample them under their feet, and turn again and rend you.
Matthew 7:6

*S*ecret #55

*E*xperience is not always the greatest teacher. Learn from other people's mistakes and successes.

#LEARNFROMOTHERS

These things happened to them as examples and were written down as warnings for us, ... – **1 Corinthians 10:11**

$\mathcal{S}$ecret #56

$\mathcal{A}$lways try to see the good in people. But never close your eyes to the possible bad inside of them.

#SEEGOODANDBADINALL

Wherefore by their fruits ye shall know them.
– Matthew 7:20

Secret #57

Leave the past where it is, in the past.
Maximize your now moment, and make it count for something great.

#MAXIMIZEYOURNOW

The righteous keep moving forward, and those with clean hands become stronger and stronger. - **Job 17:9**

Secret #58

People will always listen to you, if you have something valuable to say.
The world is longing to hear from you. Open your mouth and let your voice be heard.

#PEOPLEWILLLISTEN

A word fitly spoken is like apples of gold in pictures of silver.
– **Proverbs 25:11**

$\mathscr{S}$ecret #59

$\mathcal{D}$o not waste your words, and do not waste your time on people who are not willing to listen.

#DONOTWASTEWORDS

Fools find no pleasure in understanding, but delight in airing their own opinions. – **Proverbs 18:2**

$\mathscr{S}$ecret #60

$\mathscr{D}$o not give people the pleasure of wasting your time. Remember, if they are not pushing you to your destiny, then they are pulling you away from it.

#PUSHTOWARDSDESTINY

He that walketh with wise men shall be wise: but a **companion of fools** shall be destroyed - **Proverbs 13:20**

Secret #61

Dreams, visions and ideas are all a part of God's plan to get you safely to your destiny. Dream your dreams; see visions and put motion to your ideas.

#DREAMSVISIONSIDEAS

For I know the thoughts *and* plans that I have for you, says the Lord **Jeremiah 29:11 AMP**

Secret #62

Always read the fine print...

The things written in BOLD are usually just the advertisements.

#READTHEFINEPRINT

And in all your getting, get understanding.
Proverbs 4:7

Secret #63

Character is really who you are. Spend quality time enhancing the "better" you.

#THEBETTERYOU

The LORD will perfect that which concerns me...
- **Psalm 138:8**

$\mathcal{S}$ecret #64

$\mathcal{P}$eople will always remember who you are, more than what you do!   First impressions are lasting so leave a good memory in the minds of those you meet.

#LEAVEAGOODMEMORY

The memory of the just is blessed: ...
Proverbs 10:7

Secret #65

A little bit of hard work will not kill you.
Work hard early. You'll have time to rest, relax, and enjoy life later.

#HARDWORK

I must work the works of him that sent me, while it is day: the night cometh, when no man can work. - **John 9:4**

Secret #66

*L*earn the principles about "doors."
Just as quickly as they can open, they can also close.
If they close, seek God for wisdom as to how they can open again.

#PRINCIPLESABOUTDOORS

See, I have placed before you an open door that no one can shut.. - **Revelations 3:8**

Secret #67

Morals and principles help to govern your decisions. Life without morals is like an out-of-control train destined for a wreck, which eventually ends up nowhere.

#MORALSANDPRINCIPLES

But when He, the Spirit of Truth (the Truth-giving Spirit) comes, He will guide you into all the Truth (the whole, full Truth)- **John 16:13**

$\mathcal{S}$ecret #68

*S*et Godly standards and live by them. It is these standards by which you will always be remembered, even when the dust settles.

#GODLYSTANDARDS

All scripture is given by inspiration of God, and is profitable for doctrine, for reproof, for correction, for instruction in righteousness: – **2 Timothy 3:16**

$\mathscr{S}$ecret #69

$\mathscr{E}$very day consists of 24 hours.

You should be able to find something to smile about in at least one of the hours in your day. Smile anyway!!

#SMILEANYWAY

In everything give thanks: for this is the will of God in Christ Jesus concerning you. – **1 Thessalonians 5:18**

*S*ecret #70

*I*t is said that integrity is doing the right thing, even when nobody is looking. I believe it is also doing the right thing when everyone else around you is doing the wrong thing. To me, that's integrity!
Do the right thing all the time

#INTEGRITY

The integrity of the upright shall guide them: but the perverseness of transgressors shall destroy them.
Proverbs 11:3

Secret #71

*I*ntegrity remains outstanding ...
even under adversity and
pressure.

#OUTSTANDINGINTEGRITY

The just walketh in integrity: their children [are] blessed after them. – **Proverbs 20:7**

Secret #72

Be true to God.

Be true to yourself.

Be true to humanity.

#BETRUE

Provide things honest in the sight of all men.
– Romans 12:17

$\mathcal{S}$ecret #73

$\mathcal{A}$lways help the poor and needy.

Ignore the lazy and the greedy. Yep .... I said it! Lazy people will always try to rape, rob and leave you half dead!

#ALWAYSHELP

...It is more blessed to give than to receive
- **Acts 20:35**

Secret #74

Knowledge and understanding are powerful weapons when used with the ammunition of wisdom. Load up with lots of it and you will win every war against foolishness!

Wisdom!!!

#KNOWLEDGEWISDOMUNDERSTANDING

...Therefore get wisdom, and with all your getting get understanding... - **Proverbs 4:7**

Secret #75

*K*nowledge builds the house.

*W*isdom beautifies it.

#KNOWLEDGEBUILDSWISDOMBEAUTIFIES

Wisdom builds her house...
– Proverbs 14:1

$\mathscr{S}$ecret #76

$\mathscr{Y}$ou may have the information, but you need to know how to apply it. Wisdom is the God-given ability to successfully, accurately and effectively apply knowledge.

#APPLYINFORMATION

Wisdom is better than strength: ...
Ecclesiastes 9:16

*S*ecret #77

*C*ount your money before you sign on the "dotted line" or even before you say, "YES!"

#COUNTYOURMONEY

For which of you, intending to build a tower, sitteth not down first, and counteth the cost, whether he have sufficient to finish it? – **Luke 14:28**

Secret #78

Learn how to save, but know when to invest.
Good investments will always yield a good return.

#SAVEANDINVEST

Cast your bread upon the waters for you will find it after many days. – **Ecclesiastes 11:1**

$\mathscr{S}$ecret #79

$\mathcal{N}$ever disrespect time. If you do, time will disrespect and embarrass you...*at the wrong time!*

#ALWAYSRESPECTTIME

To every season there is a purpose and a time for everything under the heavens ... - **Ecclesiastes. 3:1**

Secret #80

Do not allow people to dump their garbage on your driveway, especially if you are planning on going somewhere.

#DONTLETPEOPLEDUMPONYOU

A good man out of the good treasure of his heart brings forth good; For out of the abundance of the heart his mouth speak -
Luke 6:45

Secret #81

*L*et people wear their own armor in warfare. Your job might just be to pray for them. The wrong armor, the wrong fight has cost many people their life.

#JUSTPRAY

"Therefore, confess your sins to one another and pray for one another ..." **– James 5:16**

Secret #82

Do not let people force you to carry them and their burden. Give them the opportunity to learn their life essential lessons or else, they will repeat the process again.

#LETPEOPLELEARN

Cast thy burden upon the LORD, and he shall sustain thee: he shall never suffer the righteous to be moved – **Proverbs 55:22**

Secret #83

Never say the words, "I CANT!" They are words of eminent defeat and failure. Always give yourself the opportunity to at least try. After you've tried at least one hundred and one (101) times, then you can walk away with peace in knowing, "YOU TRIED IT ANYHOW!"

#NEVERSAYICANT

I can do all things through Jesus Christ who strengthens me.
Philippians 4:13

Secret #84

Be careful who you give your heart to. Sometimes it's hard to get it back.

#GUARDYOURHEART

Keep (guard) your heart with all diligence for out of it flows the issues of life. – **Proverbs 4:23**

Secret #85

Seek God for wisdom!
Don't fall in love with someone you're not prepared to spend the rest of your life with.
Wait on the person who is going to love God more than they love you.
That is the one you fall in love with!!

#WAITONLOVE

Wait on the Lord and be of good courage and he shall strengthen thine heart; wait I say on the Lord. – **Psalm 27:14**

Secret #86

Don't give your heart away to anyone because you feel sorry for them.
Empathy is better than sympathy.
Learn the difference.

#SYMPATHYVSEMPATHY

This is my commandment, That ye love one another, as I have loved you. – **John 15:12**

Secret #87

*I*f you had a choice between stealing a fish and borrowing one, which would you, choose?? I would choose neither. There would still be a price to pay either way ... now or later. You would probably do better learning how to catch one yourself.

#DONTSTEALORBORROW

The rich rule over the poor; and the borrower is slave to the lender. **Proverbs 22:7**

*S*ecret #88

*I*t has often been said that a bird in the hand is better than two in a bush.
I believe the two in the bush would serve you better especially, if you know where to find them.

#ABIRDINTHEHANDISBETTER

He is a rewarder of those who diligently seek Him. –
Hebrews 11:6

*S*ecret #89

*T*his is your season of:

Double Favor.
Double Breakthrough.
Double Honor.
Enjoy every minute of every season of your life!

#YOURSEASONOFDOUBLE

Instead of your shame you will receive a double portion...You will inherit a double portion in your land and everlasting joy will be yours. – **Isaiah 61:7-8**

$\mathscr{S}$ecret #90

Change is necessary for your progress.
Be willing to adjust, especially if it is going to catapult you forward.

#CHANGEISNECESSARY

...after that ye have suffered a while, he will perfect, establish, strengthen, and settle you. - **1 Peter. 5:10**

Secret #91

Respect cannot be bought or sold
... it must be earned!

#RESPECTISEARNED

Therefore all things whatsoever ye would that men should do
to you, do you even so to them: – **Matthew 7:12**

Secret #92

Weigh all of your options before making a decision.   Let wisdom choose what's right for you.

P.S. "Wisdom is the ability to discern what is right from wrong and to know the differences between everything."

#THEWISDOMPRINCIPLE

Wisdom is the principle thing.
– Proverbs 4:7

Secret #93

A journey can be long or short. Take only that which is needed for it. Unnecessary weight will create setbacks.

#MAKETHEJOURNEY

Let us lay aside every weight, and the sin which doth so easily beset us, and let us run with patience the race that is set before us. **- Hebrews 12:1**

$\mathscr{S}$ecret #94

$\mathscr{L}$earn how to say, "NO" to people and things if it is going to take you away from your discipline.

#LEARNWHENTOSAYNO

I am saying this for your own good, not to restrict you, but that you may live in a right way in undivided devotion to the Lord.
1 Corinthians 7:35

*S*ecret #95

*D*iscipline should be one of your #1 priorities of the day. Train yourself to do that which is right. Stick to your plans unless changing them brings you closer to your goals.

#DISCIPLINEISPRIORITY

"He that [hath] no rule over his own spirit [is like] a city [that is] broken down, [and] without walls." – **Proverbs 25:28**

Secret #96

Stay S.O.B.E.R!

Never become intoxicated or drunk by anything.
People's opinion can sometimes disorient you, and if not careful, may cause nausea, dizziness, and loss of one's composure.

#STAYSOBER

Be sober, be vigilant; because[a] your adversary the devil walks about like a roaring lion, seeking whom he may devour -
1 Peter 5:8

Secret #97

*U*se the *Dr. Mattie S.O.B.E.R Module©* and you will stay on the pathway of success.

S- Structure
O- Order
B- Balance
E- Excellence
R- Regulation

P.S. Remaining **S.O.B.E.R.** will give you... Strategy, **O**rganization, **B**elief, **E**nthusiasm, and **R**ight-standing!

#THEPATHWAYOFSUCCESS

...teach the young women to be **S.O.B.E.R.** ...
– Titus 2:4

Secret #98

Drugs and alcohol tend to alter one's perception. Keep a focused eye on your destiny and goals by staying SOBER!

#FOCUSONYOURDESTINY

... if therefore thine eye be single, thy whole body shall be full of light. – **Matthew 6:22**

Secret #99

Moderation should be the order of your day!
Anything done outside of it will cause an imbalance and a warp in your scale of life.

#MODERATION

A false balance is abomination to the Lord: ...
- Proverbs 11:1

Secret #100

*P*eople are "shifty"!

Don't waste precious time trying to figure them out.
More than likely, they'll be back to their old self when the weather changes again.

#PEOPLEARESHIFTY

Do not trust a neighbor; put no confidence in a friend; wait for God your Savior; your God will hear you. – **Micah 7:5, 7**

Secret #101

Delay doesn't mean denial.

Patiently wait a while. Everything God has promised you will come to pass exactly as He said.

#DELAYISNOTDENIAL

For yet a little while, and He that shall come; will come and will not tarry. **- Hebrews 10:37**

Secret #102

Always keep your surroundings clean. Don't give anyone the "privilege" of cleaning up your mess!

#KEEPYOURAREACLEAN

The wise woman builds her house, ...
– Proverbs 14:1

Secret #103

ACCOUNTABILITY ....

*T*ake responsibility for your own actions and make others accountable for theirs!

#MAKEOTHERSRESPONSIBLE

Wherefore comfort yourselves together, and edify one another... – **1 Thessalonians. 5:11**

Secret #104

*N*ever blame people for something you had the power to change yourself.
Take responsibility for what happened.

#TAKERESPONSIBILITY

For every man shall bear his own burden.
Galatians 6:5

*L*EARN TO ...

forgive yourself and everybody else, <u>QUICKLY</u> and MOVE ON!

#FORGIVEQUICKLY

"And when ye stand praying, forgive, if ye have ought against any: that your Father also which is in heaven may forgive you your trespasses." - **Mark 11:25**

Secret #106

There are two constants in life –
God and *Change*.
In other words, God will never change, and change will always be constant.

#CHANGEISCONSTANT

"For I the LORD do not change..."
- **Malachi 3:6**

Secret #107

*N*ever believe a lie, especially when truth is looking you right in the face.

#NEVERBELIEVEALIE

Then you will know the truth, and the truth will set you free. – **John 8:32**

$\mathscr{S}$ecret #108

$\mathscr{G}$ood things come to those who wait. But greater things sometimes come to those who are willing to make it happen.

#MAKETHINGSHAPPEN

And I say unto you, Ask, and it shall be given you; seek, and ye shall find; knock, and it shall be opened unto you.
Matthew 7:7

*S*ecret #109

*M*ost people do not associate themselves with something that is "Different."
They prefer to settle with ordinary and waste time looking for the same.

#DONTSETTLEFORORDINARY

But we have this treasure in earthen vessels, that the excellency of the power may be of God, and not of us
2 Corinthians 4:7

Secret #110

*I*f you are different ... GOOD!

That's the way God made you. Accept your difference and perfect it.

#GODMADEYOUDIFFERENT

Being confident of this very thing, that he which hath begun a good work in you will perform [it] until the day of Jesus Christ.
– Philippians 1:6

Secret #111

*I*t takes the earth approximately 365 days to orbit the sun. It will take you 365 lifetimes to find someone exactly like you. In other words ... *IT WON'T HAPPEN!* Don't waste anymore time. Accept who you are as unique, and know that there is no-one else like you in the whole wide world.

#ACCEPTYOURSELF

For we are His workmanship created in Christ unto good works ... – **Ephesians 2:10**

Secret #112

Train yourself to learn quickly. If you don't get it the first time, don't be afraid to ask questions. Sometimes you have to look dumb to gain success.

#DONTBAFRAID2ASK

And shall make him of quick understanding in the fear of the Lord: ... – **Isaiah 11:3**

$\mathcal{S}$ecret #113

$\mathcal{N}$ever be afraid to stand alone, especially if it's for something you believe. The crowd is not always right.

#STANDFORWHATYOUBELIEVE

Be alert and on your guard.   Stand firm in your faith.
– 1 Corinthians 16:13

Secret #114

Do not take "NO" for an answer. Ask! And keep asking, until you get a "YES". It will be worth the struggle!

#DONTTAKENOFORANANSWER

"...ask, and ye shall receive, that your joy may be full."
– **John 16:24**

$\mathscr{S}$ecret #115

Only one insect in the world can produce real honey – and that's a honeybee. If it comes from anything else, it's an imitation. You may get stung and hear a lot of buzzing, but eventually, you will get the honey!

#GETTHEHONEY

Many are the afflictions of the righteous: but the LORD delivers us out of them all. – **Psalm 34:19**

Secret #116

On the days when you are feeling down, out, in despair and like nobody cares...
Find a bit of faith to believe God is near and He will lift you from your low place to a higher place of victory.

#GODWILLLIFTYOU

But You, O Lord, are a shield for me, my glory, and the lifter of my head. – **Psalm 3:3**

Secret #117

*I*f you are feeling sad...

Sing the "HAPPY, HAPPY, HAPPY" song when you are not feeling so happy. It will always bring a smile on your face and others.
Sad songs won't help at all.

#THEHAPPYHAPPYSONG

"My soul magnifies *and* extols the Lord; and my spirit rejoices in God my Savior." – **Luke 1:46-47**

*S*ecret #118

*S*pend quality time in prayer.

But when you cannot pray –
WORSHIP!!
Your worship creates sweet melodies from your soul – and this is a fragrance that God loves.

#THEFRAGRANCEOFYOURSOUL

"Yet a time is coming and has now come when the true worshipers will worship the Father in the Spirit and in truth..."
– John 4:23

Secret #119

Whenever you stand up to speak, sing, or dance, remember, if no-one else applauds you, GOD does and the Angels love it.
In fact, always remember, it is God you desire to please after all.

#GODSAPPLAUSE

... for the joy of the Lord is your strength.
Nehemiah 8:10

*S*ecret #120

*P*ractice, practice, practice! Hours of practice will always pay you back with favor and good success.

#PRACTICE4SUCCESS

Study to shew thyself approved unto God, a workman that needeth not to be ashamed, rightly dividing the word of truth
2 Timothy 2:5

Secret #121

*I*f you make a mistake, keep going. No-one will notice your mistakes unless you shine light on it.

#HOW2HANDLEMISTAKES

"Though he fall, he shall not be utterly cast down: for the LORD upholdeth him with his hand." – **Psalm 37:24**

Secret #122

Start strong! End strong! Always leave your audience hungry to see you again. Give them only enough to want to come back next time. Running on may lead to a dull hole you cannot get out of. Bow, leave the stage while they are applauding, crying, and celebrating the moment.

#STARTSTRONGENDSTRONG

"I press toward the mark of the higher calling found in Christ Jesus." - **Philippians 3:14**

Secret #123

Only share your story with people who are really listening and really want to hear. Don't waste your time with people who are not interested and have no appreciation for your experience.

#WHEN2TELLYOURSTORY

And they overcame him by the blood of the lamb and by the word of my testimony. – **Revelations 12:11**

Secret #124

Never tell your story for pity or sympathy.
Tell it in order to minister or make someone's life better.

#MAKESOMEONESLIFEBETTER

[No] you yourselves are our letter of recommendation (our credentials), written in [a]your hearts, to be known (perceived, recognized) and read by everybody. - **2 Corinthians 3:2(AMP)**

Secret #125

There is more than one way to solve a problem.
Seek Godly wisdom then choose the way that gets you the right answer with the
Best Results.

#GETTINGTHEBESTRESULTS

"You will seek me and find me when you seek me with all your heart." - **Jeremiah 29:13**

$\mathcal{S}$ecret #126

Short cuts and track roads are often hangouts for pirates and hijackers. Always take the right way to get the best results – even if it's the long way.

#AVOIDSHORTCUTS

Enter through the narrow gate. For wide is the gate and broad is the road that leads to destruction, and many enter through it.
Matthew 7:13

Secret #127

Starting over is not a bad idea. Especially if you discover something you did not see before. Start over, anyway and hopefully this time you will get better results.

#STARTINGOVER

... his mercies never come to an end; they are new every morning; - **Lamentations 3:22**

Secret #128

The world is filled with people who did not mind starting over again. Today they are all happy and glad they did.

#STARTINGOVERAGAIN

But grow in the grace and knowledge of our Lord and Savior Jesus Christ. - **2 Peter 3:18**

Secret #129

Always take "the calculated risk." You never know which corner success is parked on.

#THECALCULATEDRISK

Invest in seven ventures, yes, in eight; you do not know what disaster may come upon the land. – **Ecclesiastes 11:2**

Secret #130

Speak up for yourself!

Do not waste time waiting on anyone to speak up for you. After all, nobody knows you better than you!

#SPEAKUP4YOURSELF

...and [be] ready always to [give] an answer to every man that ask you a reason of the hope that is in you ... – **1 Peter 3:15-16**

Secret #131

*I*f you ever find yourself stuck or locked in a room somewhere, use whatever you have to dig yourself out. Eventually you will find a way out or better yet, someone will find you. Never sit there wallowing in self-pity.

#FINDAWAYOUT

...but with the temptation [God] will also make a way to escape, that ye may be able to bear it. – **1 Corinthians 10:13**

$\mathscr{S}$ecret #132

$\mathscr{N}$ever let your enemy or opponents see your weakness.
If you are afraid,
do what you have to do to
maintain your composure, even if
you are shaking within.

#MAINTAINYOURCOMPOSURE

Cast not away therefore your confidence, which hath great recompense of reward. – **Hebrews 10:35**

$\mathscr{S}$ecret #133

$\mathcal{E}$ven though we live in a "gender driven" society, the fact is ... you are a young lady and one day you will be a woman.
Celebrate your womanhood and strive to be the best woman you can be.

#STRIVE2BTHEBEST

Let your light so shine before men, that they may see your good works, and glorify your Father which is in heaven.
Matthew 5:16

*S*ecret #134

*D*o not allow people to devalue you. Set your standards high and maintain them.

#SETHIGHSTANDARDS

"Be thou an example of the believers, in word, in conversation, in charity, in spirit, in faith, in purity." – **1 Timothy 4:12**

Secret #135

*F*avor is better than money.

When you find it,
don't let it go.
Walk in your favor!

#FINDINGFAVOR

For whoso findeth me findeth life, and shall obtain favour of
the LORD. – **Proverbs 8:35**

*S*ecret #136

*A*lways honor and respect people, especially if they are worthy of it.

#RESPECT

Pay to all what is owed to them: ...respect to whom respect is owed, honor to whom honor is owed. – **Romans 13:7**

Secret #137

Smell good, look great, dress well, speak confidently and modestly! But whatever you do, keep the right attitude. A good character will be remembered long after your perfume wears off!

#THERIGHTATTITUDE

Be completely humble and gentle; be patient, bearing with one another in love. - **Ephesians 4:2**

*S*ecret #138

*P*eople are going to try to convince you that there are many gods. Always remember, ***there is only one! Full stop!***

#ONEGOD

Thus saith the LORD the King of Israel, and his redeemer the LORD of hosts; I [am] the first, and I [am] the last; and beside me [there is] no God. – **Isaiah 44:6**

Secret #139

Develop a good relationship with the Holy Spirit. You will find him to be a Great Teacher, Counselor, Consoler, Way Maker, Healer, Doctor, Director, Helper, Dancer, and everything else you need Him to be.

#HESEVERYTHINGYOUNEED

But the Helper, the Holy Spirit, whom the Father will send in My name, He will teach you all things ... – **John 14:26**

Secret #140

*G*o to bed in peace. Never close your eyes while you are bitter and angry at someone. Forgive, forget, pray, and then sleep!

#PEACEOFGOD

And the peace of God, which surpasses all understanding, will guard your hearts and your minds in Christ Jesus. - **Philippians 4:7**

Secret #141

Life is a series of discovery and rediscovery of yourself through the eyes of God.
Once you have discovered who you are, and why you are here; your destiny and where you are going in life becomes clear.

#LIFEDISCOVERIESANDREDISCOVERIES

Before you were born, I set you apart and appointed you... - **Jeremiah 1:5**

Secret #142

You should not waste any time waiting to be discovered by people.
Assume the position, and discover yourself with the help of God.

#DISCOVERYOURSELFINGOD

But you are ...God's special possession, that you may declare the praises of him who called you out of darkness into his wonderful light. – **1 Peter 2:9**

$\mathscr{S}$ecret #143

You are entitled to your own opinion! However, listening is a vital key to your overall success. Always be a good listener! Then spend time articulating what you have heard. Spit out the junk, swallow the good stuff, you'll grow stronger.

#LISTENINGISVITAL

Hear counsel, and receive instruction, that thou mayest be wise in thy latter end. – **Proverbs 19:20**

Secret #144

What people think and feel about you is their opinion.
What you think and feel about yourself is of greater importance.
If you think highly of yourself, others will too!

#THINKHIGHLYOFYOURSELF

For thus saith the LORD of hosts; for he that toucheth you toucheth the apple of his eye. - **Zecheriah 2:8**

Secret #145

*F*ame and money may bring you happiness but ... peace and contentment will bring you perpetual joy!

#PERPETUALJOY

Your heart shall rejoice, and your joy no man taketh from you."
- John 16:32

Secret #146

Do not change the caliber of who you really are to accommodate a season.
Remain true to yourself and God. Eventually, the season will change and accommodate you.

#REMAINTRUE2YOURSELFANDGOD

Be on your guard; stand firm in the faith; be courageous; be strong. Do everything in love. – **1 Corinthians 16:13-14**

Secret #147

Making the right choices in life protects you from impending danger. Blaming others for your repeated foolish decisions, is not only ridiculous, it's insane!

#MAKERIGHTCHOICES

Give careful thought to the paths for your feet and be steadfast in all your ways. - **Proverbs 4:26**

Secret #148

The longer you live, the more you will learn the true value of time and how to spend or manage it.

#LEARNTOVALUETIME

To every thing there is a season, and a time to every purpose under the heaven:– **Ecclesiastes 3:1**

157

$\mathcal{S}$ecret #149

$\mathcal{M}$ost young people have misconceived notions, that they have plenty of time, and if by some strange chance they run out of it, they believe they can buy more. Not So!
Wasted time can never be regained, not even on sale, not even at a thrift store.

#DONOTWASTETIME

Walk in wisdom toward them that are without, redeeming the time. – **Colossians 4:5**

Secret #150

Surround yourself with people who at least have an idea about your dreams. People who have no idea of who you are, and where you are going tend to take you in the wrong direction.

#SURROUNDYOURSELFWITHTHERIGHTPEOPLE

"Where no counsel is, the people fall: but in the multitude of counsellors there is safety." – **Proverbs 11:14**

*S*ecret #151

*A*lways surround yourself with intelligent people who at least have a grip on life.
Remove yourself from people who have no intentions of changing, growing, or developing themselves.

#THERIGHTPEOPLE

You use steel to sharpen steel, and one friend [in God] sharpens another. – **Proverbs 27:17**

Secret #152

Consult God on every matter.

Two minutes of prayer, seven times a day, will fortify your faith and give you precise direction. One dose of the Word of God, at least 3 times a day, will give you victory in everything you set your hands to do.

Try this for 21 days; you'll be shocked at the results!

#ALWAYSCONSULTGOD

... and whatsoever he (she) doeth shall prosper.
– Psalm 1:3

Secret #153

A "dead end" does not mean **"The End!"** It simply means ... turn around! God has another route to get you to your destiny.
Turn around, keep driving, and eventually you'll find the road to take you where you are going.

#ADEADENDISNOTTHEEND

... I will lead them in paths they have not known: I will make crooked paths straight before them. – **Isaiah 42:16**

Secret #154

*I*f the doors that you were suppose to go through slam shut in your face, "do not stress!" Try turning the handle on the other doors, one of them has to eventually open. This may be God's way of taking you to your divine purpose.

#DOOR2DIVINEPURPOSE

For every one that asketh receiveth; and he that seeketh findeth; and to him that knocketh it shall be opened. –
Matthew 7:8

Secret #155

College is in almost every High Achiever's dream. If you do get the chance to go, go courageously. However, if for some unforeseen reason you do not get to go, God still has a plan.

Please consider **Joseph** who did not go to college but he turned around the entire economy of Egypt. **Esther** was poor and did not have a degree but she became Queen of Shushan.

#GODSTILLHASAPLAN

Many are the plans in the mind of a man, but it is the purpose of the LORD that will stand. – **Proverbs 19:21**

Secret #156

*I*f you think you are only good for one thing, use that one thing to upgrade your status.
Upgrade your life, and help to turn someone else's life into a "good thing."

#UPGRADEYOURSTATUS

Every good and perfect gift is from above, coming down from the Father of the heavenly lights, ... - **James 1:17**

Secret #157

The thing that you think about the most, dream about the most and imagine yourself doing more than anything else in the whole world is probably what you should be doing in life!

#THETHINGYOUSHOULDBEDOING

I desire to do your will, my God; your law is within my heart. - **Psalm 40:8**

*S*ecret #158

*W*ith meticulous creativity set your own stage and dance before God. He is calling for a private audience with you... so, find quiet moments to dance before the Lord.

#DANCEB4HIM

And David danced before the Lord with all his might ...
- **2 Samuel 6:14**

Secret #159

The teacher will always be silent especially when you are going through life's hardships and tests. You will have to remember the lessons you were taught and apply them!

#EMBRACINGLIFESLESSONS

Beloved, do not think it strange, the fiery trial which is to try you, as though some strange thing happened to you ...
1 Peter 4:12

Secret #160

Whenever you are called to do something which is far greater than you, expect some level of adversity, uncertainty, complexity, and calamity. Do it anyway! People will remember you, if only for the pain you endured and the dilemmas you overcame.

#DOITANYWAY

For a great door is opened unto me, and there are many adversaries. - **1 Corinthians 16:9**

*S*ecret #161

*I*t is my belief that when you have found a cause, principle or belief outside of your own little world that you are willing to work, sacrifice and even die for-then, you have truly found your purpose!

#TRUEPURPOSE

I raised you up for this very purpose, that I might display my power in you, and that my name may be proclaimed in all the earth. – **Romans 9:17**

*S*ecret #162

*I*f you have not yet identified that "thing" which **consumes your mind, your prayers and even your finances; which keeps you up at night;** ...then I propose to you that *you have not found your purpose in life*!

#FINDINGYOURPURPOSE

For we are His workmanship created in Christ Jesus unto good works which God has before ordained that we should walk in them. - **Ephesians. 2:10**

Secret #163

Your valley experiences can cultivate in you an anointing that could never be nurtured on the mountaintop! Learn to give God praise for your valleys for therein lies your power source for life.

#MOUNTAINTOPANOINTING

Yea, though I walk through the valley of the shadow of death, I will fear no evil: ... – **Psalm 23:4**

Secret #164

*I*t is the dreams and visions that you saw before the storm that will keep you during and after the storm!

#KEEPYOURDREAMSALIVE

The vision is for an appointed time it shall speak and lie not...- **Habbakuk 2:3**

Secret #165

Whenever you encounter a victory, take two minutes and celebrate. Then, spend the other 58 minutes, in humility, digging deeper into His presence. In other words, keep your celebrations short and to the point!

#DIGDEEPER

In your presence there is fullness of joy at your right hand are pleasures forever more...you surround us with your favor Oh Lord ... – **Psalm 16:11**

*S*ecret #166

*S*owing to the winds brings back a whirlwind! Sowing into *good soil* will bring forth a good harvest!" Remember, whatever you sow, you will reap.

#THELAWOFSOWINGANDREAPING

For they have sown the wind, and they shall reap the whirlwind: **Hosea 8:8**

Secret #167

The key to the road of prosperity is not searching for a pot of gold.

It is finding a problem and solving it, finding a need and fulfilling it, finding what is broken, and fixing it.

#ROAD2PROSPERITY

But thou shalt remember the LORD thy God: for it is he that giveth thee power to get wealth ... –**Deuteronomy 8:18**

Secret #168

Never open doors you do not have the power to close. In other words, do not start something you cannot finish.

#DONTSTARTWHATYOUCANTFINISH

Be not deceived; God is not mocked: for whatsoever a man soweth, that shall he also reap. – **Galatians 6:7**

Secret #169

Do not lead people where you do not want them to follow. Only give out that which you hope to receive back. Only promise what you are able to deliver!

#DORIGHTBYOTHERS

And as ye would that men should do to you, do ye also to them likewise. – **Luke 6:31**

Secret #170

If you can trust God in the midst of the valley, you will trust him on your way to the mountaintop.

#TRUSTINGGOD

Trust in the LORD with all thine heart; and lean not unto thine own understanding ... In all thy ways acknowledge him, and he shall direct thy paths. - **Proverbs 3:5, 6**

My Book Of Secrets....

_____

_____

_____

_____

_____

_____

_____

_____

_____

_____

_____

_____

Signed: _____

And finally...whatsoever things are true,...honest,...just,...pure,... lovely,...of good report; if there be any virtue, and if there be any praise, think on these things.
Philippians 4:8

#YOURMIND#YOURTHOUGHTS#YOURWORDS #YOURACTIONS

Pre-order your copy...

"Secrets Every Mother Should Tell Her Daughter About Life!"
JOURNAL

&

"A Mother's Book of Prayers For Her Daughter"

Author of the best-selling book
"Breaking The Chains, From Worship To Warfare"

Secrets Every Mother Should Tell Her Daughter About Life

To request Dr. Mattie Nottage for a speaking engagement, upcoming event, life coaching seminar or mentorship session for girls or to place an order for products, please contact:

Mattie Nottage Ministries, Int'l (Bahamas Address)
P.O. Box SB-52524
Nassau, N. P. Bahamas
Tel/Fax: (242) 698-1383
Or (954) 237-8196

OR

Mattie Nottage Ministries, Int'l (U.S. Address)
6511 Nova Dr., Suite #193
Davie, Florida 33317

Tel/Fax: (888) 825-7568
UK Tel: 44 (0) 203371 9922

OR

www.mattienottage.org

Made in USA - Crawfordsville, IN
14118_9780989600330
02.24.2022 1241